EMPOWERED BODIES

EMPOWERED BODIES

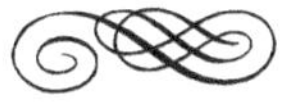

CHERRY VALENTINE

Contents

1

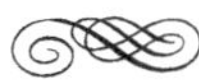

The Art of Vulnerability

Embracing the Naked Truth

Embracing the naked truth is a transformative journey that invites you to celebrate your body in its most authentic form. For OnlyFans girls, prospective nude models, E-girls, and cam girls, this journey is not just about showcasing your physical self; it's about embracing vulnerability and empowerment through artistic expression.

When you step into the realm of nude art, you begin to dismantle societal norms and redefine beauty on your own terms. Each photograph becomes a testament to your self-acceptance and a powerful declaration that your body, in all its forms, is worthy of celebration.

The beauty of collaborating with photographers who specialize in artistic nude photography lies in the shared vision of empowerment. When you work together, you create a safe space that encourages exploration and creativity. This collaboration allows you to express your individuality while also pushing the boundaries of traditional photography. Each pose, each angle, and each setting becomes a canvas for your personality, transforming the experience into a celebration of self. Embracing the naked truth means allowing yourself to be seen, not just as a model but as an artist in your own right.

Body positivity is at the heart of embracing the naked truth. It's about rejecting the unrealistic standards that often permeate the industry and accepting yourself exactly as you are. Nude photography can serve as a powerful tool for cultivating this acceptance. When you see yourself through the lens of an artist, you begin to appreciate the unique beauty that is yours alone. This process fosters a sense of community among women who share similar journeys, creating a network of support that uplifts and empowers. Every image captured is a step toward loving your body and inspiring others to do the same.

Outdoor nude photography experiences offer a unique opportunity to connect with nature while embracing your naked truth. The great outdoors serves as an expansive backdrop that enhances your experience, creating a sense of freedom and liberation. Imagine posing against a breathtaking landscape, feeling the sun on your skin, and allowing the environment to amplify your confidence. These moments can become not just photographs, but powerful memories of self-discovery and acceptance. Embracing nature in your nude art journey can deepen your connection to your body and the world around you.

Themed nude photography sessions allow you to explore different facets of your personality and express your creativity. Whether it's a whimsical fairy tale theme or a bold, edgy concept, each session can reflect a different aspect of who you are. This exploration is vital in embracing the naked truth, as it encourages you to step outside of your comfort zone and discover new dimensions of self-expression. By curating your own artistic vision, you assert your identity in a world that often tries to define it for you. Embrace the naked truth, and let your journey be a celebration of empowerment, creativity, and unabashed self-love.

Why Nude Art Matters

Nude art matters because it serves as a powerful form of self-expression that celebrates the beauty of the human body in all its forms. For those venturing into the world of nude modeling and artistic photography, embracing your nakedness can be a transformative experience. It allows you to reconnect with your body, appreciate its uniqueness, and express your individuality. In a society that often imposes unrealistic beauty standards, nude art becomes a canvas for authenticity and empowerment, inviting women to embrace their bodies and showcase their true selves.

Participating in nude art can foster a sense of community among models and photographers. When you step into a space dedicated to artistic exploration, you're not just working; you're engaging in a dialogue about body positivity and self-acceptance. Collaborating with photographers who prioritize artistic vision over mere objectification creates a safe environment where everyone involved feels valued and respected. This mutual respect enhances the creative process, resulting in stunning imagery that celebrates both the art form and the individuals within it.

Moreover, nude art challenges societal norms around nudity and sexuality. It pushes boundaries and invites conversations about what it means to be comfortable in one's skin. For those involved in platforms like OnlyFans or as cam girls, engaging in nude art can redefine personal branding. It allows you to curate a visual narrative that aligns with your values and artistic vision, showcasing your confidence and creativity. By presenting yourself in an artistic light, you invite your audience to see you as more than just a body; you become a storyteller, an artist, and a muse.

Outdoor nude photography experiences offer a unique opportunity to connect with nature while celebrating the human form. The juxtaposition of the naked body against the natural landscape creates breathtaking visuals and deepens the appreciation for both art and environment. Being in nature while embracing nudity can be liberating, allowing you to truly feel at one with the earth. These experiences can also foster a profound sense of empowerment, as you challenge societal taboos and embrace your body in its most vulnerable state.

Finally, themed nude photography sessions provide an exciting avenue for creativity and exploration. Whether it's a vintage pin-up theme or a fantasy-inspired shoot, these sessions allow you to express different facets of your personality while celebrating your body. Themed shoots can also foster a sense of playfulness and freedom, encouraging you to step outside your comfort zone and explore new artistic avenues. By participating in these creative endeavors, you not only empower yourself but also inspire others to embrace their bodies and explore the beauty of nude art in all its forms.

The Power of Collaboration in Nude Photography

Collaboration is a transformative force in the realm of nude photography, where creativity meets empowerment. For OnlyFans girls, prospective nude models, e-girls, and cam girls, the opportunity to collaborate with photographers can elevate the art of self-expression to new heights. When two or more individuals come together, they create a synergy that can capture the essence of vulnerability, strength, and beauty. Each participant brings their unique perspective, experiences, and style to the table, resulting in images that resonate on a deeper emotional level. This partnership not only enhances the final product but also fosters a sense of community and shared purpose.

In the journey of exploring artistic nude photography, collaboration can provide a safe space for models to express their individuality. By working together, both the photographer and the model can discuss their visions, themes, and comfort levels, ensuring a respectful and empowering environment. This dialogue is crucial for establishing trust, which allows for genuine connections to flourish. The result? Stunning photographs that reflect not just the physical form, but also the personality and spirit of the model. A collaborative approach transforms the shoot into a co-creative experience where everyone feels valued and heard.

Body positivity is a vital theme in nude photography, and collaboration helps amplify this message. When models come together with photographers who prioritize inclusivity and body diversity, the resulting images challenge societal norms and celebrate all forms of beauty. This movement empowers models to embrace their bodies, regardless of shape, size, or background. By showcasing a variety of bodies in an artistic context, collaborative nude photography promotes a narrative of acceptance and self-love that resonates with audiences around the world. Each image becomes a powerful statement, encouraging others to embrace their own uniqueness.

Outdoor nude photography experiences offer yet another avenue for collaboration that can heighten the thrill and authenticity of the art. Nature provides a stunning backdrop that enhances the beauty of the human form, and working together in such settings can amplify the feelings of freedom and empowerment. Whether it's a serene forest, a rocky beach, or an open field, the natural environment invites a sense of adventure and spontaneity. Collaborating in these spaces allows models and photographers to experiment with poses, angles, and themes that reflect their personal branding while connecting with the world around them.

Themed nude photography sessions are another exciting area where collaboration shines. These sessions can range from whimsical to dramatic, allowing for endless creative possibilities. By brainstorming ideas together, models can take an active role in shaping the narrative and aesthetic of the shoot. This kind of creative partnership not only leads to breathtaking imagery but also strengthens the bond between the collaborators. The process of exploring different themes, concepts, and styles encourages both the model and photographer to step outside their comfort zones, leading to personal growth and artistic development. Ultimately, the power of collaboration in nude photography is about celebrating self and fostering a community that uplifts and empowers everyone involved.

2

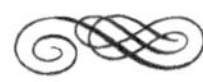

Building Trust:
Asking for the Shot

How to Approach Potential Models

Approaching potential models for nude art photography can be an exhilarating experience, filled with creative possibilities and opportunities for empowerment. When reaching out to individuals, especially those in the OnlyFans community or aspiring nude models, it's crucial to emphasize the artistic vision behind the project. Begin by expressing your passion for celebrating the human form through art and how their unique beauty can contribute to this journey. Highlight the collaborative nature of the process, ensuring they understand that their comfort and consent are paramount. This sets a positive tone for the conversation and reassures them that they will be integral to the creation of the artwork.

To make your approach more engaging, consider personalizing your outreach. Take the time to research the individuals you wish to collaborate with and reference their existing work or online presence. This not only shows genuine interest but also helps build a connection. Share your enthusiasm about their style and how it aligns with your vision. Whether it's their vibrant personality as an e-girl or the confidence they exude as a cam girl, acknowledging their strengths creates a more inviting atmosphere for discussion. Your excitement can be contagious, inspiring them to join you on this artistic adventure.

Once you have established a rapport, discuss the concept of body positivity and empowerment through nude art. Explain how this collaboration can serve as a platform for exploring and celebrating their bodies in a safe and supportive environment. Share stories of past projects that have helped models embrace their self-image, highlighting the transformative power of intimate photography. This can help to alleviate any apprehensions they may have about posing nude, reinforcing that the experience is not only artistic but also affirming and liberating.

Safety and comfort should be at the forefront of your approach. Clearly outline the measures you will take to create a secure space for the photoshoot, whether it's a private studio or an outdoor location. Discuss your commitment to maintaining confidentiality and respecting boundaries throughout the process. Offer the option to bring a friend or advocate along, ensuring they feel supported. By prioritizing their well-being, you demonstrate that your project values more than just aesthetics; it values the model's experience and feelings.

Lastly, invite potential models to share their ideas and visions for the shoot. Encourage them to express any themes or concepts they are passionate about, whether it's a whimsical outdoor setting or a powerful statement on self-expression. This collaborative approach fosters a sense of ownership over their representation in the art. By creating an environment where their voice is heard, you not only enhance the artistic outcome but also empower them to embrace their bodies and celebrate their individuality. Together, you can embark on a journey of self-discovery through the lens of artistic nude photography.

Setting the Right Tone for Consent

Setting the right tone for consent is essential in the world of nude art, where we celebrate the beauty and empowerment of our bodies. As creators and models in this vibrant community, establishing a clear and respectful dialogue about consent is the foundation of every successful collaboration. It's about creating an atmosphere where everyone feels comfortable, valued, and excited to express themselves. When you prioritize consent, you're not just protecting yourself—you're fostering creativity and artistic expression that allows everyone involved to shine.

In this world, consent goes beyond a simple agreement; it's a dynamic conversation that continues even after the initial discussions. As an OnlyFans girl, prospective nude model, or cam girl, you have the power to shape the narrative around your body and how it's portrayed. Use your voice to articulate your boundaries, preferences, and desires. Whether it's through intimate photography for personal branding or themed nude photography sessions, maintaining open channels of communication ensures that everyone is on the same page, creating a collaborative environment rich with trust and creativity.

Empowerment through nude art thrives when all parties feel safe and respected. Establishing safe spaces for nude photography exploration means being proactive about consent, discussing it openly, and incorporating it into every aspect of your shoots. This includes not only the initial agreement but also ongoing check-ins during the session. Encourage your collaborators to express their feelings, and don't hesitate to voice yours.

This mutual respect transforms the experience into something truly magical, allowing for genuine connections to flourish and artistic visions to come alive.

Body positivity is a crucial element in the conversation about consent. As you navigate the world of artistic nude photography, remember that every body deserves admiration and respect. When you approach consent with a body-positive mindset, you empower not just yourself but also those around you. Celebrate the diversity of bodies and perspectives, and encourage your peers to embrace their uniqueness. This collective empowerment creates a ripple effect, inspiring others to join in the celebration of self through art, breaking down barriers, and challenging societal norms in the process.

Lastly, let's not forget the thrill of outdoor nude photography experiences. These sessions can be exhilarating and liberating, but they also require a nuanced understanding of consent, especially in shared public spaces. Be mindful of your surroundings and the comfort levels of everyone involved. Discuss what to expect, establish clear boundaries, and reassure each other that your comfort comes first. By setting the right tone for consent, you're not only enhancing your own experience; you're also paving the way for a more inclusive and joyful community that embraces the beauty of the human form in all its diverse expressions.

Creating an Empowering Invitation

Creating an empowering invitation is a key step in establishing a collaborative and positive atmosphere for nude art photography. Whether you are reaching out to prospective nude models, e-girls, or cam girls, the essence of your invitation should resonate with empowerment and creativity. Start by expressing your passion for the art form and the transformative power it holds. Make it clear that your intention is not just to capture images, but to celebrate the beauty of the human body and to foster a space where everyone feels valued, respected, and free to express themselves.

When crafting your invitation, emphasize the collaborative nature of the project. Highlight that this is a partnership where both parties contribute ideas, concepts, and energy. Encourage potential collaborators to bring their own visions to the table, whether that means suggesting themes, locations, or styles. This co-creative process will not only enhance the artistic outcome but also empower the models by giving them agency in how they are portrayed. Celebrate the idea that every body tells a unique story, and invite them to share theirs through the lens of your camera.

In addition to artistic collaboration, it's vital to address the importance of creating a safe space for exploration. Reassure those you invite that your environment is one of trust and respect. Be clear about your commitment to ethical practices, emphasizing confidentiality and consent throughout the process. Acknowledge that many individuals may have apprehensions about nude photography, and provide reassurances that their comfort and boundaries will always be prioritized. This openness will help in building a rapport that fosters genuine connection and creativity.

Moreover, consider incorporating themes that resonate with body positivity and self-acceptance. Your invitation can serve as a powerful statement that challenges societal norms and celebrates diversity in all its forms. Encourage potential collaborators to embrace their unique beauty, regardless of shape, size, or background. By framing your project within the context of body positivity, you are not only inviting models to participate but also inviting them to embark on a personal journey of self-love and acceptance. This aspect can be particularly empowering for those involved, transforming the experience into a celebration of individuality.

Finally, don't forget to convey the joy and excitement that comes with the experience of nude art photography. Whether it's an outdoor adventure or a themed session, highlight the fun and liberating aspects of the process. Create a sense of anticipation by sharing your vision for the shoot and what participants can expect. Ignite their imagination by painting a vivid picture of the creative possibilities that lie ahead. An enthusiastic invitation will not only attract the right individuals but also set the tone for a memorable experience that celebrates self-expression and empowerment through the art of the nude.

3

The Magic of Collaboration

Co-Creating Art: A Shared Vision

Co-creating art is an exhilarating journey that transcends the mere act of photographing the human form. For OnlyFans creators, prospective nude models, and cam girls, this collaboration can become a powerful expression of shared vision, where each participant brings their unique energy, ideas, and creativity to the table. Artistic nude photography is not just about capturing a moment; it is about creating a collaborative experience that celebrates vulnerability, authenticity, and empowerment. When you engage with photographers who understand this dynamic, you can transform your body into a canvas that tells your story while embracing your individuality.

Imagine stepping into a space where your comfort and creativity are prioritized. This is the essence of co-creating art—it's about building trust and establishing an environment that allows you to explore and express yourself freely. As you collaborate with photographers, communicate your desires, boundaries, and inspirations. This dialogue not only enhances the artistic process but also fosters a sense of empowerment. You are not just a subject; you are an integral part of the creative vision, shaping the narrative through your body language, expressions, and energy. Together, you can push the boundaries of traditional nude photography, crafting images that resonate with authenticity and personal significance.

Body positivity plays a crucial role in this collaborative art-making process. By embracing your body in all its forms, you challenge societal norms and celebrate diversity. When you co-create with photographers who advocate for body positivity, you reinforce the idea that every body is worthy of being celebrated and captured beautifully. This shared vision empowers you to reclaim your narrative and showcase the beauty that lies within your unique self. The images produced through this partnership not only represent artistic expression but also serve as powerful statements of self-love and acceptance, inspiring others to embrace their bodies as well.

Exploring intimate photography for personal branding can also benefit immensely from this collaborative approach. Working together with a photographer, you can curate a visual story that aligns with your brand while highlighting your personality and style. Themed nude photography sessions offer an exciting avenue for creativity, allowing you to experiment with concepts that resonate with you. Whether it's a nature-inspired shoot or a fantasy-themed exploration, the collaboration enables you to express different facets of your identity and engage your audience on a deeper level.

Outdoor nude photography experiences can be some of the most liberating and empowering ventures. The natural environment serves as a backdrop that amplifies the beauty of the human form, encouraging you to connect with nature and your own body. Co-creating in these spaces allows for a sense of freedom and spontaneity, resulting in stunning imagery that captures the essence of both the landscape and your spirit. By engaging in these collaborative projects, you not only produce breathtaking art but also contribute to a growing movement that celebrates the beauty of the human body in all its forms. Embrace the opportunity to co-create, share your vision, and revel in the empowerment that comes from showcasing your authentic self through art.

Celebrating Diversity: Every Body is Beautiful

Celebrating diversity in body types is not just a trend; it's a revolution that empowers individuals to embrace their unique forms and express themselves through the art of nudity. In a world that often perpetuates narrow standards of beauty, it is vital to recognize that every body is a canvas, worthy of admiration and celebration. Whether you are an OnlyFans girl, a prospective nude model, or an E-girl exploring your identity, understanding the beauty of diversity allows you to connect with your audience on a deeper level. This connection fosters authenticity, encouraging you to share your true self with the world.

When you step in front of the camera, you are not just presenting your body; you are telling a story that reflects your experiences, struggles, and triumphs. Each pose, every curve, and the way light dances across your skin is an opportunity to showcase your individuality. Artistic nude photography is a powerful medium that allows for this expression, breaking down societal norms and celebrating the beauty in differences. Through collaboration with skilled photographers, you can create striking images that not only highlight your features but also convey a message of body positivity and acceptance.

Engaging in themed nude photography sessions can further amplify your message. These experiences can vary from whimsical and playful to deeply personal and introspective. By curating themes that resonate with you, you can inspire others to embrace their own bodies in all their forms. Imagine exploring the outdoors in an intimate photography session, where nature serves as a backdrop to your celebration of self. Such settings can enhance the narrative of body positivity, reinforcing that beauty exists in every environment and every body.

Creating safe spaces for nude photography exploration is essential for fostering a supportive community. As you connect with fellow models and photographers, you establish an environment where everyone feels respected and valued. This sense of security allows for genuine expression and creativity to flourish, enabling you to explore your comfort zones and push boundaries. When you collaborate with others who share your vision of empowerment through nude art, you amplify the message that every body is beautiful, and every story deserves to be told.

Ultimately, celebrating diversity in the nude art realm is about embracing authenticity and self-love. As you embark on your journey as a nude model or content creator, remember that your body is a beautiful representation of your unique story. By showcasing your individuality and supporting others in their journeys, you contribute to a larger movement that challenges conventional beauty standards and celebrates every body. Together, let's pave the way for a future where all bodies are celebrated, cherished, and empowered through the art of nudity.

The Role of Communication in Artistic Partnerships

Artistic partnerships in nude photography thrive on effective communication, serving as the backbone of creativity and collaboration. For Onlyfans girls, prospective nude models, and e-girls, establishing a clear dialogue with photographers and fellow artists is essential. This communication not only sets the tone for the artistic vision but also ensures that everyone involved feels respected, empowered, and aligned in their intentions. When artists openly express their ideas, preferences, and boundaries, they create a collaborative environment where creativity can flourish. This open line of communication can lead to stunning visuals that reflect the unique essence of each participant, making every project a true celebration of self.

Understanding each other's creative processes is another crucial aspect of communication in artistic partnerships. Every model and photographer brings their own style, perspective, and set of experiences to the table. By discussing these elements upfront, both parties can discover how their visions can intertwine. For instance, a model might share her interest in body positivity, while a photographer might have a flair for outdoor settings. By communicating these interests, they can brainstorm themed sessions that highlight their strengths and passions, resulting in artwork that resonates deeply with their audiences. This synergy not only enhances the artistic output but also fosters a sense of community and support within the nude art space.

Trust is fundamental in any artistic collaboration, particularly in the realm of nude photography. Clear and honest communication builds this trust, allowing models to feel safe and valued throughout the creative process. It's essential to establish guidelines around comfort levels and boundaries, ensuring that everyone knows what is acceptable. This is especially important for models who may be new to the experience. When photographers take the time to listen and engage in meaningful conversations about comfort and consent, it creates a safe space for exploration and expression. The result is a more authentic and empowered representation of the human body, captured in a way that honors each individual's uniqueness.

Moreover, effective communication can significantly enhance the branding efforts of those involved in nude art. For e-girls and cam girls, understanding how to articulate their artistic vision and personal brand can lead to unique opportunities in the online space. By collaborating with photographers who align with their aesthetic and values, they can create compelling images that resonate with their audience. These visuals serve not just as art but as powerful branding tools that convey confidence, creativity, and authenticity. Communicating openly about goals and expectations enables models to curate a portfolio that truly reflects who they are, drawing in a community that appreciates their individuality.

Finally, communication cultivates a mindset of empowerment within artistic partnerships. As models and photographers share their ideas and experiences, they inspire one another to push boundaries and explore new territories in nude art. This exchange of perspectives enriches the creative process, leading to innovative concepts and unforgettable sessions. Whether it's planning an adventurous outdoor shoot or delving into intimate themed photography, the dialogue between collaborators ignites a passion that transforms their work into something extraordinary. Embracing communication as a vital component of artistic partnerships not only enhances the quality of the art produced but also solidifies a supportive community that celebrates and uplifts every participant's journey in the world of nude art.

4

Empowerment Through Artistic Expression

Finding Strength in Vulnerability

Finding strength in vulnerability is a transformative journey, especially for those of us navigating the world of nude art and self-expression. When stepping in front of the camera, shedding clothing can feel like shedding layers of societal expectations, fears, and insecurities. It's here, in this raw exposure, that we discover a profound sense of empowerment. By embracing our vulnerabilities, we invite others to do the same, creating a ripple effect that fosters community and connection among us.

Vulnerability is often seen as a weakness, but in the realm of nude photography, it becomes a powerful tool for self-acceptance and body positivity. Each click of the shutter captures not just our physical form but also the essence of who we are. By allowing ourselves to be seen in our most authentic state, we challenge traditional beauty standards and redefine what it means to be beautiful. This act of bravery encourages others to step into their own light, creating a safe space for diverse bodies and stories to flourish.

Artistic nude photography offers a unique opportunity to explore and celebrate our bodies in ways that can be both liberating and healing. Through collaboration with photographers, we can communicate our stories and express ourselves artistically. This collaboration can break down barriers, allowing us to share our vulnerabilities while crafting compelling narratives that resonate with others. The trust built between model and photographer can lead to stunning imagery that reflects our inner strength, showcasing the beauty in our imperfections.

Outdoor nude photography experiences add an exhilarating layer to this exploration. The natural world becomes a backdrop for our authenticity, encouraging us to connect with our bodies and the environment around us. Each outdoor session is an invitation to let go of inhibitions and immerse ourselves in the moment. The combination of nature and vulnerability fosters a sense of freedom, reminding us that our bodies are not only beautiful but also deserving of celebration in all settings.

Ultimately, finding strength in vulnerability is about embracing who we are, inside and out. As we share our journeys through intimate photography, we inspire others to embark on their own paths of self-discovery. In doing so, we cultivate a community rooted in acceptance, support, and empowerment. By celebrating our bodies through nude art, we not only reclaim our narratives but also empower others to find their strength in vulnerability, creating a legacy of confidence and self-love that will resonate far beyond the frame.

Transforming Self-Perception Through Art

Transforming self-perception through art is a journey that resonates deeply with those who embrace their bodies and celebrate their unique identities. For Onlyfans girls, prospective nude models, e-girls, and cam girls, engaging with artistic nude photography offers a powerful avenue for personal empowerment. When you step in front of the camera, you are not just posing; you are making a bold statement about your body and your worth. This transformative experience allows you to connect with your inner self, shedding layers of insecurity and embracing the beauty of vulnerability.

Artistic nude photography serves as a mirror, reflecting not only your physical form but also your emotional landscape. Each click of the shutter captures your essence, revealing the strength and confidence that may have been hidden beneath societal expectations. This process can be exhilarating and liberating, as it encourages you to redefine how you see yourself. By collaborating with photographers who appreciate the artistry of the nude form, you create a safe space to explore your body positively, fostering an environment where self-love and acceptance flourish.

Body positivity is at the heart of this transformative journey. In a world that often dictates unrealistic standards of beauty, nude art celebrates diversity and individuality. Every curve, scar, and freckle tells a story, and through artistic expression, you can reclaim your narrative. Engaging in themed nude photography sessions or outdoor experiences allows you to explore different facets of your personality while amplifying your unique beauty. This celebration of self can inspire others in your community, encouraging them to embrace their bodies and express themselves fearlessly.

The connection forged between the model and the photographer is essential in this artistic process. When both parties approach the collaboration with mutual respect and understanding, the magic unfolds. This relationship transforms into a dance of creativity, where ideas flow freely, and boundaries are respected. The result is a collection of images that not only enhance your personal brand but also serve as a testament to your journey of self-discovery and empowerment. Each photograph becomes a reminder of your strength, resilience, and willingness to embrace your authentic self.

Ultimately, transforming self-perception through art is about more than just the final images; it's about the experience and growth along the way. As you embark on this artistic journey, remember to celebrate every moment. Engage in the process, connect with your body, and relish the freedom that comes from expressing yourself authentically. The power of artistic nude photography lies not only in its visual impact but also in its ability to inspire confidence and foster a community where every body is celebrated. Embrace this opportunity, and let your art transform the way you perceive yourself and the world around you!

Stories of Empowerment: Models Share Their Journeys

In the world of nude art, empowerment transcends mere aesthetics; it embodies the journeys of individuals who embrace their bodies and share their stories through the lens of a camera. For many models, stepping into the realm of nude photography is a transformative experience that allows them to reclaim their narratives and celebrate their identities. These women come from diverse backgrounds, but they all share a common thread: a desire to express themselves authentically and empower others to do the same. Their stories not only inspire but also create a community where body positivity and self-love flourish.

Take, for example, the journey of Mia, a former corporate worker who found herself stifled by traditional beauty standards. After discovering the world of artistic nude photography, she decided to embark on a new path. With each photoshoot, Mia learned to appreciate her body in ways she never thought possible. The camera became her ally, capturing her vulnerability and strength simultaneously. Through her experience, she has encouraged fellow women to embrace their natural forms, proving that beauty lies in authenticity. Mia's story exemplifies how nude art can serve as a powerful tool for self-discovery and empowerment.

Then there's Lila, a thriving OnlyFans creator who uses her platform to promote body positivity and self-expression. Lila's journey began as a personal exploration of her sexuality and self-worth. As she delved deeper into the world of nude modeling, she began to realize that her influence reached far beyond her own experiences. Lila has created themed photography sessions that challenge societal norms and celebrate diversity. By sharing her story and showcasing her art, she empowers other women to take ownership of their bodies and redefine what it means to be beautiful. Her work illustrates the impact of intimate photography on personal branding and the importance of creating safe spaces for self-exploration.

Another inspiring tale is that of Zoe, who ventured into outdoor nude photography as a way to connect with nature and herself. For Zoe, the experience was about shedding not just clothes but also the societal expectations that had burdened her for years. Each session in the great outdoors allowed her to embrace her body in its most natural form, surrounded by the beauty of the world. Through her journey, Zoe highlights the importance of context in nude art, emphasizing how the environment can enhance the empowerment experience. Her story encourages other women to seek out similar experiences, reinforcing that vulnerability in nature can lead to profound self-acceptance.

Lastly, we have Jasmine, who turned to artistic nude photography as a means of healing after a personal trauma. Her journey is a testament to the therapeutic potential of self-expression through art. With the support of compassionate photographers and a nurturing community, Jasmine discovered the strength that lies within her scars. Each photograph tells a story of resilience and courage, inviting others to find solace in their own vulnerabilities. Her experience showcases how intimate photography can be a powerful catalyst for healing, encouraging women to embrace their bodies and share their journeys with pride.

These narratives of empowerment reflect the transformative power of nude art, making it a vital aspect of self-expression for many women. By sharing their journeys, Mia, Lila, Zoe, and Jasmine not only celebrate their bodies but also inspire others to explore their own paths of empowerment. In a world that often seeks to define beauty through narrow lenses, these models challenge the status quo, inviting women everywhere to embrace their uniqueness. Their stories serve as a reminder that every body has a story worth telling, and through artistic nude photography, those stories can be celebrated and empowered.

5

Body Positivity in Focus

Challenging Societal Norms

Challenging societal norms is an exhilarating journey that invites us to redefine our identities through the lens of our bodies. For OnlyFans girls, prospective nude models, e-girls, and cam girls, this path is not just about disrobing; it's about embracing vulnerability and celebrating authenticity. By stepping into the world of nude art, we can shatter stereotypes, challenge outdated perceptions of beauty, and reclaim ownership of our bodies. Each photograph becomes a statement, a powerful declaration that our bodies are worthy of admiration and expression, no matter their shape or size.

Artistic nude photography collaboration provides a unique platform for women to come together and create magic. When we collaborate, we not only share our visions but also foster a sense of community that uplifts and empowers. As we work with photographers who understand the nuances of body positivity, we can craft images that resonate deeply with our individuality. These sessions are more than just artistic endeavors; they are safe spaces where we can explore our bodies, challenge societal expectations, and showcase the beauty that often goes unnoticed. The process itself becomes a celebration, where each click of the camera captures our strength and vulnerability in equal measure.

Empowerment through nude art is about more than aesthetics; it's about embracing our stories and showcasing them through our bodies.

Each scar, stretch mark, and curve tells a tale, and when we allow ourselves to be seen in our most authentic form, we inspire others to do the same. This act of self-acceptance fuels a movement toward body positivity, encouraging women everywhere to love themselves fiercely. In a world that often tries to dictate how we should look and behave, choosing to express ourselves through nude art is a radical act of defiance and liberation.

Outdoor nude photography experiences offer an exhilarating way to connect with nature while challenging societal norms. Imagine basking in the sunlight, surrounded by breathtaking landscapes, and feeling free to express your body in ways that feel empowering. The natural world provides a stunning backdrop that enhances the beauty of our forms, reminding us that we are part of something greater. These experiences not only celebrate our bodies but also encourage us to appreciate the world around us, reinforcing the idea that our existence is intertwined with nature's splendor.

Themed nude photography sessions take this empowerment further by allowing us to explore different facets of our identities. Whether it's embodying a character, channeling an emotion, or expressing a personal narrative, these sessions enable us to break free from the confines of societal expectations. They invite creativity and self-exploration, transforming our bodies into canvases that tell our stories. By challenging societal norms through these artistic expressions, we pave the way for a future where every body is celebrated, and every woman feels empowered to embrace her true self.

Celebrating All Bodies in Nude Photography

Celebrating all bodies in nude photography is a powerful movement that invites everyone to embrace their unique forms and stories. For OnlyFans girls, prospective nude models, e-girls, and cam girls, this art form transcends mere visuals; it becomes a celebration of self-acceptance and body positivity. Every curve, scar, and mark tells a story, and through the lens of a camera, these stories can be expressed in their most authentic form. This is not just about showcasing the body but about reclaiming it, transforming vulnerability into strength, and turning everyday insecurities into sources of pride.

In the realm of artistic nude photography, collaboration is key. Working with a photographer who values your vision and understands the importance of consent can lead to breathtaking results. This partnership creates a safe space where both model and photographer can explore the depths of creativity. Whether you choose to convey a narrative through your poses or simply let your body speak for itself, the collaboration becomes a canvas for empowerment. The energy shared during these sessions often ignites confidence and fosters a sense of community, reminding us that we are not alone in our journeys.

Body positivity is at the heart of celebrating all bodies in nude photography. This art form challenges societal norms that dictate what is deemed beautiful or acceptable. By showcasing diverse bodies, we create a tapestry of representation that helps dismantle harmful stereotypes. Every body is worthy of being celebrated, regardless of size, shape, color, or age. As you step in front of the camera, remember that you are part of a larger movement that advocates for acceptance and love in all forms. Your image can inspire others to embrace their bodies and recognize their beauty, paving the way for a more inclusive future.

Outdoor nude photography experiences add an exciting layer to the celebration of bodies. The natural world becomes an intimate backdrop, allowing for a connection between the model and the environment. This setting not only enhances the artistic expression but also encourages a sense of freedom and liberation. Imagine the thrill of feeling the sun on your skin or the gentle breeze as you pose amidst nature's beauty. These moments can deepen your appreciation for your body and its place in the world, turning each photograph into a celebration of life itself.

Themed nude photography sessions offer another avenue for creative exploration and self-expression. Whether it's a vintage-inspired shoot, a fantasy theme, or an exploration of cultural motifs, these sessions invite you to embody different personas and narratives. Engaging in such experiences can be incredibly empowering, allowing you to step outside your comfort zone and discover new facets of yourself. Surrounding yourself with supportive photographers and fellow models in these safe spaces creates an atmosphere of encouragement, fostering a community where every body is honored and celebrated, and where the journey towards self-love and acceptance is shared.

The Impact of Body Positivity on Self-Confidence

The body positivity movement has made significant strides in reshaping societal norms around beauty and self-acceptance. For those in the realms of nude art and personal branding, this paradigm shift offers an empowering foundation for self-confidence. As OnlyFans girls, prospective nude models, and cam girls, embracing body positivity can unlock authentic expressions of self, allowing you to showcase your unique beauty in a world that often promotes unrealistic standards. When you celebrate your body as it is, you not only enhance your own self-worth but inspire others to do the same, creating a ripple effect of confidence among your peers.

Engaging in artistic nude photography is an act of self-love and defiance against conventional beauty ideals. When you step in front of the camera, particularly in intimate or outdoor settings, you are embracing vulnerability while simultaneously reclaiming your narrative. This experience can be transformative; it encourages you to view your body not as an object of judgment but as a canvas of expression. Every curve, every scar, every mark tells a story, and by sharing that story through art, you elevate your self-confidence and invite others to appreciate the beauty of imperfection.

Body positivity fosters a sense of community among those in the nude photography space. By collaborating with other artists and models, you create safe environments where everyone feels valued and respected. This collective embrace of diverse body types and narratives adds depth to artistic expression, allowing for more authentic and relatable content. As you work together, you not only uplift one another but also challenge the stigma around body image, reinforcing the idea that beauty exists in all forms. In these safe spaces, confidence flourishes, and the bonds created can lead to lifelong friendships and support systems.

Moreover, the impact of body positivity extends beyond the camera lens. As you cultivate self-confidence, it spills over into other aspects of your life, enhancing your personal brand and online presence. When you exude confidence, it resonates with your audience, drawing them in and fostering a deeper connection. Your authenticity becomes your greatest asset, allowing you to stand out in a crowded digital landscape. This newfound assurance can also transform the way you approach your work, whether it's through themed sessions or casual outdoor shoots, encouraging you to take risks and explore new creative avenues.

Ultimately, the celebration of body positivity within the nude art community is a powerful catalyst for self-empowerment. By embracing your body and encouraging others to do the same, you contribute to a larger movement that values authenticity over perfection. This journey not only enhances your self-confidence but also challenges societal norms, paving the way for a future where all bodies are celebrated. As you navigate your path in this vibrant world, remember that your confidence is a beacon that shines brightly, inspiring others to join you in celebrating the beauty of empowered bodies.

6

Intimacy and Branding

Using Nude Art for Personal Branding

Using nude art for personal branding can be a transformative experience, allowing you to celebrate your body and express your individuality. In the world of OnlyFans, camming, and modeling, standing out is essential. By embracing your own unique beauty through artistic nude photography, you not only create stunning visuals but also communicate a powerful message of self-acceptance and empowerment. Each photograph tells a story, a narrative that conveys your personality, values, and creative vision, making it a vital tool in establishing your brand.

Collaborating with photographers who specialize in artistic nude work can elevate your brand to new heights. This partnership can bring fresh ideas and perspectives, resulting in stunning images that capture your essence. The synergy between model and photographer often leads to extraordinary results, where both parties contribute to the creative process. Trust is key, so finding a safe space where you feel comfortable is crucial. A supportive environment fosters creativity, allowing you to express yourself freely and authentically, which ultimately shines through in your work.

Body positivity is at the heart of using nude art for personal branding. By showcasing your body in its natural form, you challenge societal norms and inspire others to embrace their own imperfections. This celebration of diversity not only resonates with your audience but also establishes you as a role model in the body positivity movement. Your brand can become synonymous with acceptance and love, encouraging others to join you in this empowering journey. As you share your art, you inspire a community that values authenticity over unrealistic standards.

Outdoor nude photography experiences can add a thrilling dimension to your personal brand. Nature provides a stunning backdrop that enhances the beauty of your photographs while creating a sense of freedom and connection to the earth. Imagine the exhilaration of posing amidst breathtaking landscapes, where every shot encapsulates the rawness of the moment. These sessions can be both liberating and invigorating, allowing you to explore your body in ways you might never have imagined, all while capturing captivating images that resonate with your audience.

Themed nude photography sessions can further amplify your personal branding strategy. Whether it's a vintage-inspired shoot, a fantasy concept, or a celebration of cultural heritage, themed sessions allow you to express different facets of your personality. By curating a specific aesthetic or message, you engage your audience on multiple levels, inviting them to connect with your brand in a more profound way. These creative explorations not only diversify your portfolio but also create memorable experiences that your followers will cherish. Embrace the artistry of nude photography, and let it propel your personal brand into new realms of empowerment and celebration.

Crafting Your Unique Identity Through Photography

Crafting your unique identity through photography is an exhilarating journey that allows you to express your individuality in the most intimate and empowering way. For those in the realms of OnlyFans, aspiring nude models, and e-girls, embracing your naked form in front of the camera can be a transformative experience. It's not just about showcasing your body; it's about celebrating who you are, what you stand for, and how you desire to be seen in the world. Each click of the shutter captures more than just an image;

it encapsulates your essence, your story, and your raw beauty.

Artistic nude photography is a powerful medium for self-expression that encourages body positivity and self-acceptance. By collaborating with photographers who understand your vision, you can create stunning visuals that highlight your unique identity. Think about the themes you want to explore—whether it's confidence, vulnerability, or empowerment. Every session offers an opportunity to delve deeper into your persona, allowing you to emerge from the experience with a stronger sense of self. Your body is a canvas, and through the lens, you can paint it in the most authentic colors.

Outdoor nude photography experiences add an exhilarating twist to this journey. Imagine the thrill of shedding your clothes and embracing nature, surrounded by breathtaking landscapes that complement your form. These sessions can foster a profound sense of freedom and connection with the environment, enhancing the narrative you want to convey. The natural light, the wind on your skin, and the sounds of the outdoors can create an unforgettable atmosphere that amplifies your authenticity. It's in these moments that you can truly discover the power of your body and the beauty of your identity.

Themed nude photography sessions can also be a delightful way to explore and express different facets of your personality. Whether it's a vintage pin-up vibe, a fantasy-inspired shoot, or a modern artistic portrayal, these themes offer endless opportunities for creativity. Collaborating with photographers who share your enthusiasm for these concepts can lead to remarkable results. Each theme not only showcases your body but also tells a story, allowing you to engage with your audience on a deeper level. This fusion of art and identity can elevate your personal brand and set you apart in a crowded space.

Creating safe spaces for nude photography exploration is essential in fostering an environment where you feel empowered to fully express yourself. When you work with professionals who prioritize comfort and respect, you can explore your identity without fear or judgment. This safety is crucial for authentic expression, allowing you to push boundaries and discover new aspects of yourself. Remember, your body is your own, and how you choose to present it is a powerful statement. By embracing the art of nude photography, you are not just crafting images; you are crafting a narrative that celebrates your unique identity and empowers your journey.

The Balance of Intimacy and Professionalism

In the world of nude art, striking the right balance between intimacy and professionalism is essential for fostering an empowering environment. This delicate equilibrium allows models to feel safe and celebrated while also ensuring that the artistic vision is respected and achieved. As you navigate this vibrant landscape, remember that intimacy does not have to compromise professionalism; instead, they can complement each other beautifully. Embrace this synergy, and watch as it transforms your experience, enhancing both the artistry and the personal connections you cultivate.

Building a space where intimacy thrives starts with establishing trust and open communication. As models, you have the power to voice your boundaries and preferences, creating a collaborative atmosphere that encourages creativity. When photographers and models engage in candid conversations about desires, inspirations, and comfort levels, the result is often extraordinary. This level of interaction not only enriches the artistic process but also fosters an environment where everyone feels valued and heard. Remember, the essence of your body and spirit shines through when you feel supported and understood.

Professionalism in nude photography involves treating the art and the individuals involved with respect and integrity. It is crucial to set clear expectations regarding the shoot, including logistics, themes, and the intended use of the images. This clarity helps to create a productive space where artistry can flourish without misunderstandings. When both parties approach the collaboration with a professional mindset, it elevates the work produced and deepens the bonds formed during the process. Your empowerment as a model comes from knowing that your body is not only a canvas but a significant part of a larger, meaningful conversation about art and identity.

In the realm of body positivity, this balance becomes even more crucial. Celebrating diverse bodies through nude art requires a commitment to creating an inclusive environment where all forms of beauty are appreciated. When intimacy and professionalism coexist, models can express themselves authentically without fear of judgment. This powerful dynamic encourages individuals to embrace their unique figures and inspire others to do the same. As you embark on this journey, remember that your contributions to body positivity are vital, and your confidence radiates when you feel both intimate and professional in your craft.

Outdoor and themed nude photography sessions offer unique opportunities to explore this balance further. The natural world provides a stunning backdrop for artistic expression, while thematic elements can enhance the narrative of your work. In these settings, the connection between the model and the environment can evoke profound emotions and a sense of freedom. However, it is essential to maintain professionalism by ensuring safety and comfort throughout the experience. By creating safe spaces for exploration, you empower not only yourself but also others within the community to celebrate their bodies and express their artistry boldly and confidently.

7

Outdoor Adventures: Nature as a Canvas

Choosing the Perfect Outdoor Location

Choosing the perfect outdoor location for your nude photography session is an exhilarating adventure that can significantly enhance your artistic expression and personal empowerment. The great outdoors offers an infinite variety of backdrops, from serene forests and sandy beaches to vibrant urban landscapes. Each setting brings its own unique energy and aesthetic, which can amplify the themes you wish to explore in your art. Imagine the feeling of freedom as you pose under the open sky, surrounded by nature, or the exhilarating contrast of your body against a bustling cityscape. The right location not only boosts your confidence but also sets the tone for the entire shoot, making the experience unforgettable.

When selecting an outdoor location, consider the vibe you want to convey. Are you drawn to the tranquility of a secluded meadow, where the gentle rustling of leaves can be your soundtrack? Or perhaps a rugged mountain backdrop that symbolizes strength and resilience speaks to you? Think about the emotions and stories you want to express through your body and the art you create. Each location can evoke different feelings, and choosing one that resonates with your message will elevate your art and empower you as a model. The connection you build with your surroundings will shine through in the photographs, creating a more authentic representation of you.

It's also essential to think about accessibility and comfort when choosing your outdoor setting. Look for locations that are not only visually stunning but also safe and easy to reach. Whether it's a popular park, a hidden gem in nature, or a specific urban spot, ensure that it allows for privacy and comfort as you embrace your body in its natural state. Safety should always be a priority, so scout locations during different times of the day to assess the foot traffic and lighting. This way, you can choose a time that minimizes interruptions and maximizes your creative flow.

Another aspect to consider is the time of day and the natural light available in your chosen location. The golden hour, just after sunrise or before sunset, offers soft, flattering light that can transform your images into breathtaking works of art. This magical time enhances skin tones and creates beautiful shadows, highlighting your body's contours. Experiment with different times and weather conditions to see how they affect your desired outcome. Understanding how light interacts with your environment can lead to striking photographs that capture the essence of empowerment and body positivity.

Lastly, always remember to embrace spontaneity. Sometimes the most magical moments happen when you least expect them. As you explore your chosen location, allow yourself to be inspired by the surroundings. Engage with the environment, whether it's using natural elements as props or allowing a breeze to dictate your poses. This flexibility can lead to a more authentic and dynamic photo shoot, celebrating not just your body, but the beauty of the world around you. By choosing a location that speaks to you and encourages exploration, you empower yourself and others, showcasing the incredible journey of self-acceptance through nude art.

The Therapeutic Benefits of Nature

The therapeutic benefits of nature are profound, especially when intertwined with the art of nude photography. For those in the realms of OnlyFans, cam modeling, and artistic nude photography, embracing the natural world can enhance both personal well-being and creative expression. Imagine stepping into a sun-drenched forest or a serene beach, shedding the layers of everyday life, and allowing the beauty of your body to connect with the beauty of the earth. This synergy not only fosters a sense of empowerment but also cultivates a deep appreciation for one's own form in a natural setting, reminding us that we are part of something larger.

Nature has an incredible way of grounding us, offering a space where we can explore our bodies without judgment. For prospective nude models and e-girls, the outdoors provides a canvas rich with textures, colors, and light that can elevate the experience of intimate photography. Posing amidst the elements—whether it's the gentle rustle of leaves or the sound of waves crashing—can inspire confidence and authenticity. This connection to the environment encourages a flow of creativity that often results in stunning imagery, showcasing the raw beauty of the human form in harmony with nature.

Embracing nature also promotes body positivity, a vital theme for those involved in nude art.

When you immerse yourself outdoors, you can cultivate a mindset that celebrates your body, regardless of societal standards. The natural world reflects diversity in its landscapes and ecosystems, mirroring the uniqueness of every individual. This acceptance can be incredibly liberating, allowing models to view their bodies as beautiful and worthy of being celebrated. By engaging in outdoor nude photography experiences, you not only challenge personal insecurities but also inspire others to embrace their bodies through the lens of nature's splendor.

Themed nude photography sessions in natural settings can further enhance this journey of empowerment. Whether it's a whimsical fairy tale forest or a dramatic cliffside overlooking the ocean, each theme can tell a story that resonates deeply with the viewer. Collaborating with fellow artists and photographers in these settings can create a safe space for exploration and expression. It's within these shared experiences that models can find support and encouragement, transforming the act of being photographed into a celebration of individuality and strength.

Ultimately, the therapeutic benefits of nature are not just about the stunning visuals; they are about the profound connection to oneself and the environment. For those in the nude art community, stepping outside can be a transformative experience that fosters empowerment, creativity, and body positivity. As we celebrate self through nude art, let us remember to honor the natural world that surrounds us, allowing it to inspire and uplift us in our artistic endeavors. Embrace the outdoors, connect with your body, and let the beauty of nature serve as a backdrop for your personal journey of self-discovery and expression.

Capturing the Essence of Freedom

Capturing the essence of freedom through nude art is an exhilarating journey that invites individuals to explore their bodies and express their true selves. For OnlyFans girls, prospective nude models, e-girls, and cam girls, this exploration is not just about the physical form but also about shedding societal constraints and embracing authenticity. In each captured moment, there lies a powerful narrative that celebrates individuality, confidence, and the beauty of vulnerability. The act of posing nude becomes a declaration of autonomy, allowing women to reclaim their bodies and their stories in a world that often seeks to define them.

The process of artistic nude photography collaboration is an empowering experience that fosters creativity and connection. Working with photographers who respect and understand the nuances of body positivity transforms every session into an opportunity to celebrate imperfections and uniqueness. By creating a safe space, both the model and the photographer can engage in an open dialogue about vision, comfort, and boundaries. This collaboration allows for a genuine expression that transcends mere visuals, capturing the essence of freedom that comes from being unapologetically oneself.

Outdoor nude photography experiences further amplify the feeling of liberation, as nature serves as a backdrop that enhances the raw beauty of the human form. The elements—the sun, wind, and earth—become partners in the art, creating a dynamic interplay of light and shadow that highlights the body in its most natural state. This setting encourages models to connect with their surroundings, embracing the thrill of vulnerability while surrounded by the vastness of the world. Each shot taken outdoors is infused with a sense of adventure, reinforcing the notion that freedom is also about breaking free from conventional confines.

Themed nude photography sessions add a playful layer to this exploration of freedom, allowing models to express different facets of their personalities. Whether embodying a whimsical character or channeling inner strength, these sessions encourage creativity and self-discovery. The themes can evoke various emotions, from empowerment to sensuality, and provide a unique platform for models to tell their stories visually. When women step into these roles, they not only celebrate their bodies but also inspire others to embrace their own narratives, reinforcing the bond of sisterhood in the nude art community.

Ultimately, capturing the essence of freedom through nude art is about creating a movement rooted in self-love and acceptance. It's a celebration of the diverse bodies that exist and a reminder that every curve, scar, and imperfection tells a story worth sharing. For those engaged in this art form, the journey is not just about the images produced but about the transformation that occurs along the way. With every click of the shutter, a new chapter is written, and a new understanding of freedom is forged, inspiring countless others to embark on their own journeys of empowerment through nude art.

8

Creative Themes for Nude Sessions

Exploring Fantasy and Role Play

Exploring the realms of fantasy and role play within the context of nude art opens up a vibrant world of self-expression and creativity. For OnlyFans girls, prospective nude models, and cam girls, this exploration serves as a powerful tool to engage with your audience on a deeper level. By incorporating themed elements into your nude photography sessions, you can transform ordinary images into captivating narratives that resonate with viewers. Whether you're embodying a fairy tale character, a mythological figure, or a unique persona of your own design, the possibilities are as limitless as your imagination.

Role play in nude art not only enhances the aesthetic appeal of your work but also fosters a sense of empowerment. Embracing different characters allows you to step outside your everyday self and explore aspects of your personality that may remain hidden. This transformative experience is not just liberating; it encourages body positivity by celebrating all forms and identities. By showcasing your body in diverse roles, you challenge societal norms and redefine beauty standards, inviting others to view themselves through a more accepting lens.

Creating safe spaces for nude photography exploration is crucial for this journey. Whether you're collaborating with a photographer or working on your own projects, establishing an environment where you feel comfortable and supported is essential. This atmosphere encourages vulnerability, allowing you to delve into your fantasies without fear of judgment. Communicate openly with your collaborators about your vision, boundaries, and desires, ensuring that everyone involved shares the same commitment to respect and creativity.

Outdoor nude photography experiences further amplify the thrill of role play. Imagine capturing the essence of nature while embodying a character that resonates with the surroundings. The interplay of light, landscape, and your chosen persona can create breathtaking images that tell a story. Consider themed sessions inspired by seasonal changes, local folklore, or even your favorite books and movies. Each shoot can become an adventure, allowing you to connect with nature and your audience simultaneously.

Ultimately, exploring fantasy and role play in nude art is about more than just creating visually stunning content; it's about celebrating your individuality and empowering others to do the same. Every photograph becomes a testament to the beauty of self-exploration, encouraging women to embrace their bodies and express themselves freely. As you embark on this journey, remember that your creativity knows no bounds, and each image you produce is a powerful declaration of self-love and artistic expression.

Themed Costumes and Accessories

Themed costumes and accessories in nude art can transform a standard photoshoot into an exhilarating celebration of creativity and self-expression. For those of you navigating the world of Onlyfans, modeling, or camming, embracing themed costumes allows you to showcase your unique personality while exploring the beautiful concept of nudity. Imagine stepping into a fantasy world where you can embody characters or concepts that resonate with you, all while feeling empowered in your own skin. This approach not only enhances the visual narrative of your work but also invites your audience to engage with your art on a deeper level.

When selecting a theme, think about what excites you personally. Whether it's a vintage pin-up look, a whimsical fairytale character, or a modern-day superhero, your choices can reflect your passions and interests. Accessories play a pivotal role in this transformation. A simple crown, a feather boa, or even a pair of statement earrings can elevate the entire shoot, adding layers of meaning and intrigue. These items can serve as conversation starters, allowing you to connect with your audience and share the stories behind your choices, thus fostering a deeper connection through your artistic expression.

Working with a photographer who understands your vision is essential for bringing your themed costume ideas to life. Collaborating on artistic nude photography can create a safe space for experimentation and exploration. Discussing your ideas openly can lead to innovative approaches and unexpected outcomes. The right photographer will not only respect your boundaries but will also help you feel comfortable and empowered, allowing your true self to shine through the lens. This partnership can be a rewarding experience, nurturing creativity and building confidence as you step into the roles you've envisioned.

Outdoor themed nude photography sessions add an exciting element to the mix. Imagine capturing your artistic expression against the backdrop of nature, where the beauty of your body blends seamlessly with the environment. Whether it's a lush forest, a serene beach, or an urban setting, outdoor photography offers unparalleled opportunities for creativity. The natural light and scenery can enhance your chosen theme, making the images even more striking while promoting body positivity and celebration of self. Embracing this dynamic setting allows you to break free from traditional studio constraints and immerse yourself in a liberating experience.

Ultimately, themed costumes and accessories in nude art are about empowerment, self-discovery, and body positivity. Every piece you wear or accessory you choose is a reflection of your journey and an invitation for others to appreciate the beauty of diversity in body shapes and sizes. By embracing your individuality and exploring different themes, you create a powerful statement about self-love and acceptance. Each photoshoot becomes not just a moment in time but a bold declaration of your identity, encouraging others to celebrate their own bodies in all their forms. So, unleash your creativity, let your imagination run wild, and watch as your confidence soars with every themed session you embark upon.

Telling Stories Through Themed Sessions

Telling stories through themed sessions is an exhilarating way to embrace and celebrate the beauty of the human form while crafting a narrative that resonates with both the model and the audience. Each session presents an opportunity to explore different facets of identity, emotions, and creativity. Whether it's a whimsical fairy tale or a raw exploration of vulnerability, themed sessions allow models to step into diverse roles and express themselves authentically. This form of artistic collaboration invites everyone involved to contribute ideas, making the experience not just a photoshoot, but a shared journey into self-discovery and empowerment.

Imagine stepping into a world where every detail, from costumes to props, helps narrate a story that you want to tell. Themed sessions can be tailored to reflect personal experiences or fantasies, allowing models to connect deeply with their art. This connection is vital—it transforms the experience from merely posing for the camera into a powerful act of self-expression. When you're fully immersed in a theme that resonates with you, the authenticity shines through in the images, creating a visual narrative that speaks volumes about who you are and what you want to convey.

Moreover, themed sessions cultivate a sense of community and support among models and photographers. They create safe spaces where individuals can explore their bodies and identities without judgment. In these encouraging environments, models can experiment with different poses, expressions, and styles, enhancing their confidence and comfort in front of the camera. When you collaborate on a themed project, you're not just sharing a space; you're sharing stories and experiences that uplift and inspire each other. This collective creativity can lead to breathtaking results that celebrate diversity and body positivity in nude art.

Incorporating elements from various themes can also open doors to innovative concepts that challenge conventional ideas of beauty. For instance, you might blend classical art influences with modern aesthetics, creating a stunning juxtaposition that highlights the timelessness of the human form. Outdoor themed sessions can harness the natural beauty of the environment, where sunlight and landscapes become essential components of the story. Each photograph can capture more than just a moment; it can encapsulate the essence of empowerment and freedom, celebrating bodies in all their forms.

Ultimately, telling stories through themed sessions is not just about capturing images; it's about creating a powerful dialogue around self-acceptance and empowerment. Every photo becomes a testament to individuality and strength, encouraging others to embrace their own bodies and stories. For OnlyFans girls, prospective nude models, e-girls, and cam girls, these sessions can be a vital part of personal branding, showing the world the unique narratives that each of you carries. So, gather your creative ideas, connect with like-minded individuals, and embark on this artistic adventure that celebrates who you are in the most beautiful and empowering way possible!

9

Creating Safe Spaces for Exploration

Establishing Comfort and Safety in Sessions

Establishing an environment of comfort and safety is paramount in any session that celebrates the beauty of the human body through nude art. For OnlyFans girls, prospective nude models, and e-girls, creating this atmosphere not only enhances the experience but also empowers individuals to express themselves freely. When you walk into a session feeling secure and accepted, it sets the stage for creativity to flourish. This chapter will explore practical approaches to ensure that you and your collaborators can focus on showcasing your authentic selves without anxiety or hesitation.

First and foremost, communication is the key to establishing comfort. Prior to the session, discuss your comfort levels, boundaries, and expectations with everyone involved. This is not just about discussing poses and locations; it's about sharing personal limits and preferences. When everyone is on the same page, it cultivates an atmosphere of respect and understanding. Encourage an open dialogue where everyone feels empowered to voice their thoughts and concerns. This foundational step fosters trust and ensures that everyone feels safe to express their individuality and creativity during the shoot.

Creating a physical space that reflects safety and comfort can significantly enhance the experience. Whether you're shooting indoors or outdoors, pay attention to the environment. Soft lighting, warm colors, and inviting props can help set a relaxed mood. If you're in a more open set-ting, consider using natural elements like blan-kets or cushions to create intimate spaces. These small touches can transform a space into a sanc-tuary where you feel encouraged to explore artis-tic expressions. Additionally, consider the temperature of the location—keeping it comfort-able will allow you to focus on the art rather than any discomfort.

Another crucial aspect is to set the tone through positive reinforcement and support. As you collaborate with others, uplift each other through affirmations and encouragement. Cele-brate the beauty of diverse body types and the unique stories that each participant brings to the session. This not only boosts confidence but also reinforces the message of body positivity that is central to nude art. When everyone feels appreci-ated and valued, it creates a vibrant atmosphere where creativity can thrive, allowing for stunning artistic expressions that celebrate each body's story.

Lastly, always prioritize consent and respect throughout the shoot. Establish clear guidelines regarding what is acceptable and what is not, and be sure that everyone involved understands the importance of these boundaries. Consent should be an ongoing conversation, not just a checkbox. This practice not only protects everyone's comfort but also enhances the artistic collaboration. By making safety a shared priority, you empower yourself and others to fully engage in the experience, resulting in art that is not only beautiful but also deeply meaningful. Embrace these principles, and you will cultivate an enriching environment that honors and celebrates the power of nude art.

Nurturing a Supportive Environment

Creating a nurturing and supportive environment is essential for any nude art endeavor, particularly for those venturing into the world of artistic expression through their bodies. For Onlyfans girls, prospective nude models, and cam girls, the atmosphere in which you work can significantly affect your comfort, confidence, and creativity. A supportive environment not only encourages self-expression but also fosters a sense of community and empowerment. When you feel safe and valued, your artistry can truly shine, allowing your unique beauty to take center stage.

Establishing this supportive environment begins with open communication. Whether you're collaborating with photographers or fellow models, discussing your boundaries, preferences, and expectations is crucial. This dialogue not only builds trust but also ensures that everyone involved feels respected and heard. For those engaging in artistic nude photography, sharing your vision and insights with your collaborators can lead to stunning results that capture the essence of your individuality. Remember, your voice is powerful; use it to shape your experience and create art that resonates deeply.

Another vital aspect of nurturing a supportive environment is the importance of body positivity. Embracing diverse body types and celebrating uniqueness can transform your experience in the nude art realm. Surround yourself with individuals who uplift and inspire you, focusing on the beauty of each body rather than adhering to societal norms. This mindset creates a ripple effect, encouraging everyone to appreciate their own forms and enhancing the overall atmosphere of acceptance. Together, you can challenge conventional beauty standards, paving the way for a more inclusive representation of the human body.

Safety is paramount in any artistic exploration, especially in the realm of nude photography. Establishing safe spaces where models can express themselves without fear of judgment or exploitation is crucial. This could be a physical location, like a studio that prioritizes comfort and security, or an online community where you can share experiences and advice. Ensure that consent is always prioritized, and that everyone understands the significance of mutual respect. When you cultivate an environment where safety is guaranteed, creativity flourishes, and the beauty of vulnerability can be explored without hesitation.

Lastly, embracing themed nude photography sessions can serve as a catalyst for creativity and connection. These sessions allow you to explore various aspects of your identity and artistic vision while collaborating with like-minded individuals. Whether it's an outdoor shoot that taps into nature's beauty or a conceptual theme that challenges societal norms, these experiences can deepen your understanding of self. By nurturing a supportive space, you are not only celebrating your own body but also empowering others to do the same. Together, you can create art that inspires, uplifts, and transforms perceptions of nudity and self-expression.

Respecting Boundaries and Personal Comfort

Respecting boundaries and personal comfort is a cornerstone of creating empowering and transformative experiences in the realm of nude art. For women engaged in this vibrant world, whether as OnlyFans creators, prospective nude models, e-girls, or cam girls, establishing and communicating personal boundaries is essential. Each individual has her unique comfort zones, and recognizing these limits is not only respectful but also vital for fostering a healthy environment. Embracing your own comfort and encouraging others to do the same can enhance the collaborative spirit of artistic nude photography, allowing for authentic expressions of self.

When considering collaborations in artistic nude photography, take the time to have open and honest discussions about boundaries and expectations. This dialogue is crucial in ensuring that all participants feel safe and valued. Discuss what each person is comfortable with regarding poses, settings, and themes, and be willing to reassess these agreements as the creative process unfolds. Remember, flexibility is key. The more you communicate, the more empowered everyone will feel, resulting in a more enriching experience that celebrates the beauty of the human body in artistic form.

Body positivity plays a significant role in the world of nude photography. It's imperative to cultivate an atmosphere that uplifts and affirms all body types, shapes, and sizes. When you respect your own boundaries, you set a powerful example for others. Encourage those around you to embrace their bodies and to express themselves freely without fear of judgment or criticism. This approach not only enhances the artistic process but also promotes a broader culture of acceptance and love for one's own body. In this way, personal comfort becomes a collective celebration of diversity and empowerment within the nude art community.

Creating safe spaces for nude photography exploration is another essential aspect of this journey. Whether you're participating in outdoor nude photography experiences or themed sessions, the environment should feel secure and welcoming. This means selecting locations where everyone feels at ease, both physically and emotionally. It might involve scouting locations ahead of time, discussing potential concerns, or even establishing safe words or signals during a shoot. Prioritizing comfort ensures that creativity can flow freely and that the resulting art reflects genuine expression rather than hesitation or discomfort.

Ultimately, respecting boundaries and personal comfort is an empowering practice that enriches the experience of engaging in nude art. It invites open dialogue, fosters body positivity, and cultivates safe spaces for exploration. By tak-

ing these principles to heart, you not only enhance your artistic endeavors but also contribute
to a supportive community where every individual can thrive. Embrace the journey of self-expression, knowing that by honoring your own
comfort and that of others, you are championing
a movement that celebrates the beauty and power
of the human form in all its diversity.

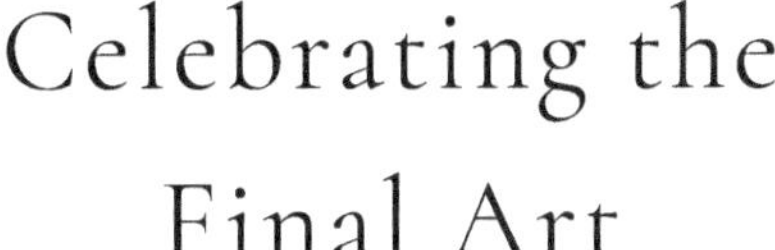

Celebrating the Final Art

Showcasing Your Work: Exhibitions and Social Media

Showcasing your work is a vital aspect of building your brand and connecting with your audience, especially in the realm of nude art. Exhibitions and social media provide incredible platforms for you to display your creativity and celebrate your body in an empowering way.

Whether you're participating in a live exhibition or posting stunning images online, these opportunities allow you to engage with like-minded individuals who appreciate the beauty of self-expression through artistic nude photography. Embrace the chance to share your journey and inspire others with your unique perspective on body positivity.

Participating in exhibitions can be an exhilarating experience, offering you the chance to display your work in a physical space where art lovers gather. Seek out local galleries that focus on body positivity or artistic nude photography, and consider collaborating with fellow artists or photographers who share your vision. This not only expands your network but also fosters a sense of community among those who celebrate the beauty of the human form. An exhibition can be a transformative experience, allowing you to connect with your audience on a deeper level, sparking conversations around empowerment, vulnerability, and the importance of self-love.

Social media serves as a powerful tool for showcasing your work and reaching a global audience. Platforms like Instagram, TikTok, and Twitter enable you to share your artistic journey, engage with fans, and connect with other models and photographers in the nude art community. Use captivating captions and hashtags to draw attention to your posts, highlighting the themes of empowerment and body positivity that resonate with your audience. Regularly updating your profile with fresh content keeps your followers engaged and encourages them to share your work, further amplifying your reach and impact.

When sharing your work online, consider the narrative you want to convey. Each photo should tell a story, whether it's about embracing your body, exploring personal themes, or celebrating the beauty of intimacy. Create themed series that reflect different aspects of your identity or experiences, allowing your audience to connect with you on a personal level. Engaging in discussions about the themes represented in your art can foster a sense of belonging among your followers and encourage them to share their own stories of empowerment through nude art.

Finally, prioritize creating safe spaces for exploration and expression, both in your exhibitions and online platforms. Encourage open dialogue and community support, where individuals can feel comfortable sharing their experiences and insights. Whether it's through curated online groups or intimate in-person gatherings, fostering an environment of acceptance will empower others to embrace their bodies and appreciate the beauty of artistic nude photography. By showcasing your work authentically, you not only celebrate your own journey but also inspire others to explore their own self-expression and reclaim their narratives through art.

Empowering Others Through Shared Art

The journey of exploring and celebrating our bodies through art is not just a personal endeavor; it's a powerful collective experience that can uplift and empower others in the community. When you step into the realm of nude art, you are not merely exposing your physical form; you are sharing a message of confidence, self-love, and authenticity. This shared experience can inspire those around you—whether they are fellow models, photographers, or fans—encouraging them to embrace their own bodies and stories. By collaborating with others in artistic nude photography, you create a space where everyone feels valued and seen, fostering a sense of belonging and empowerment.

Imagine the magic that happens when you invite someone to participate in a nude art session. This act can ignite a spark of creativity that transcends the individual. Through shared artistic pursuits, you can help others discover their comfort zones and challenge societal norms. The experience of posing alongside others or even stepping behind the camera can be a transformative journey. Encouraging your peers to explore their bodies through the lens of art can lead to profound moments of self-discovery, making them feel powerful and liberated. This collaborative spirit cultivates a community where everyone can embrace their vulnerabilities together, turning them into strengths.

Artistic nude photography is a beautiful medium for promoting body positivity. By showcasing diverse bodies in all their forms, you help redefine beauty standards and highlight that every body is worthy of celebration. This movement toward inclusivity is essential, especially in a world that often imposes unrealistic ideals. When you share your art—whether through social media or exhibitions—you send a message that resonates with those who may feel marginalized. It empowers others to see themselves in the art and appreciate their unique beauty. Your journey can inspire countless women to love themselves fiercely and unapologetically, creating a ripple effect that extends beyond the canvas.

Creating safe spaces for nude photography exploration is vital in this process. It's crucial to establish environments where participants feel comfortable and respected. When everyone involved understands the importance of consent and boundaries, it opens the door to deeper connections and more authentic expressions. Whether you're organizing themed sessions or outdoor experiences, prioritizing safety and comfort can elevate the artistic process. This sense of security encourages models to express themselves freely, resulting in breathtaking images that convey genuine emotions and stories. By building these inclusive spaces, you become a beacon of empowerment for others.

Ultimately, the beauty of empowering others through shared art lies in its ability to foster connections and build communities. Every photograph tells a story, and by collaborating with others, you create a tapestry of experiences that showcases the richness of human expression. As you navigate your artistic journey, remember that your voice and body have the power to inspire others. Celebrate the strength found in vulnerability, and encourage those around you to embrace their own narratives. Together, through the lens of artistic nude photography, you can create a movement that not only empowers individuals but also nurtures a vibrant community where everyone feels celebrated and uplifted.

Leaving a Lasting Impact with Your Photography

Photography has the unique power to capture not just images but emotions, stories, and the essence of who we are. For those venturing into the world of nude art, especially within the vibrant spaces of OnlyFans, cam modeling, and artistic collaborations, every photograph becomes a statement. It's a celebration of the body, a declaration of self-love, and a platform for empowerment. When you step in front of the camera or collaborate with photographers, remember that your presence can inspire others to embrace their own bodies and stories, creating a ripple effect that extends far beyond the frame.

Each photograph you share can be a beacon of positivity, encouraging viewers to appreciate diversity in body shapes, sizes, and colors. By showcasing your unique beauty, you challenge societal norms and redefine standards of attractiveness. This powerful act can inspire others, especially those who may struggle with body image issues, to see themselves in a new light. Emphasizing body positivity through your work not only empowers you but also uplifts those who view your art, fostering a community that celebrates individuality and authenticity.

Collaboration is at the heart of artistic nude photography. Working with photographers, fellow models, or artists can lead to groundbreaking projects that leave a lasting impression. Consider themed shoots that explore various narratives or concepts, allowing you to express different facets of your identity and creativity. These collaborations can result in stunning visuals that provoke thought and conversation, making your work memorable and impactful. Building a network of like-minded individuals not only enhances your artistic journey but also strengthens the movement toward body acceptance and empowerment.

Outdoor nude photography experiences can take your art to an entirely new level. The natural environment provides a stunning backdrop that emphasizes the beauty of the human form in harmony with nature. These sessions can evoke feelings of freedom and connection, allowing you to express vulnerability and strength simultaneously. When you share these intimate moments, you invite your audience to appreciate the beauty of both the body and the world around us, reinforcing the message that we are all part of a larger tapestry of life.

Creating safe spaces for nude photography exploration is essential for fostering confidence and authenticity. Whether you're working in a studio or outdoors, prioritizing comfort and consent ensures that every participant feels valued and respected. By advocating for safe environments, you encourage open dialogue about body image and self-expression, making it easier for others to share their stories. Remember, the impact of your photography extends beyond the visual; it resonates deeply with emotions and experiences, shaping how individuals view themselves and their bodies. Your art can create waves of change, inspiring a movement of acceptance and empowerment that lasts long after the final click of the shutter.

www.ingramcontent.com/pod-product-compliance
Lightning Source LLC
Chambersburg PA
CBHW071337140726
47996CB00005B/2022